Conversations with a Dead Lover

poems by

Maryrose Carroll

Finishing Line Press
Georgetown, Kentucky

Conversations with a Dead Lover

ACKNOWLEDGMENTS

With sincere appreciation I wish to acknowledge the advice, collaboration and
stupendous encouragement given by my friends, the poets,

Dan Champion,
Earl LeClare, and
Joseph Bathanti, North Carolina Poet Laureate, 2013-14.

Publisher: Leah Maines

Editor: Christen Kincaid

Cover Art: Maryrose Carroll

Author Photo: Maryrose Carroll

Interior Photos and Artwork: Maryrose Carroll

Cover Design: Elizabeth Maines McCleavy

Printed in the USA on acid-free paper.
Order online: www.finishinglinepress.com
also available on amazon.com

Author inquiries and mail orders:
Finishing Line Press
P. O. Box 1626
Georgetown, Kentucky 40324
U. S. A.

Table of Contents

For Paul Carroll... always my beginning...

Photo of Paul Carroll, 1958, Paul D. Carroll Papers, Special
Collections Research Center, University of Chicago Library.

Prologue

"Twelve months, at the most," he said, softly, his words buzzing in my ears like hornets. Looking at this kind, dark-eyed doctor, with unexpected anger, suddenly, I hated him. In his white coat and khaki cowboy boots, he had, at last, offered the truth we had trudged, from doctor to doctor, fearing to hear. Dr. DeVirgillis was the only one to successfully diagnose my husband's symptoms—lack of energy, stomach discomfort, and impotency— as terminal bladder cancer. It wasn't his fault Paul was dying. The bounty of Paul's life-long cigarette habit couldn't be escaped. "Arsenic," he told me. "tobacco deposits arsenic in the bladder."

Leaving the examination room dressed in his spiffy dark-green, corduroy pants, wing-tipped shoes, Paul, looked, ironically, like a dude. However, he walked stooped over like a curse had been dumped on his back. What were we going to do with this wretched news? How was I going to care for my husband as he relentlessly edged closer to death? How was I going to live without his love, without hearing his new poems, without cuddling in bed, spoon fashion? I didn't have a blasted clue. I had only dreamed about having such love in my life and, now, this doctor threatened to whisk it all away. How could I not hate him?

As I drove home from the doctor's office, in Boone, up over George's Gap, we traveled in uncustomary silence to our farm. When we moved here, Paul and I became the first resident non-Ellers, an extended family that built and occupied this two story, white clapboard house for one hundred years. Our property is tucked in the eastern face of the last ridge before Stone Mountains, marking the state line between North Carolina and Tennessee. Our whistling, Little Beaver Dam Creek, fronting the public side of the farm, feeds into Beaver Dam Creek and then the Watauga River.

The first two months of living with a death sentence were ghastly silent. We were not our usual garrulous selves. Paul, was certainly well known as a great story teller, with a superb memory, knowledge of poets, writers, football players. One of his poems praised "football weather". But depression, a ghost from his past, had swooped in seizing the opportunity. I feared that his current lack of appetite or interest in life, low energy would continue all twelve months. I was at a loss as how to revive his spirits, especially since he was now impotent. But, a miracle happened! An angel of life must have visited him in the night because suddenly he woke one morning and was back his gabby, happy self.

He simply told me that he realized all he could do was "to live one day at a time." Thank God!

We resumed our sunset ritual. When the weather was kind, Paul and I loved to move out from the house to sit under the Chinese chestnut trees framing the creek to sip our wine and talk. He said the creek sometimes sounds like jazzman Bix Beiderbecke's cornet. We talked about his new poem "Last Will and Testament," in which he wills his heart to me, his brains to his son, Luke, and wills his feet "to anyone who wants to flee bigotry and superstition."

Our path through his last twelve months proceeded with miraculously little pain for Paul. In the final six months, he would ask visiting hospice nurses, "How can I have cancer if I have no pain?" But the inevitable progress of the disease was invisibly at work. By the tenth month, when he read his poems at the dedication of my sculpture in Charlotte's social services building, he had lost twenty pounds. Yet his delivery was superb and one lady in the audience wanted to know if he would return the following week.

Labor Day weekend, in his 11th month, he took a dramatic turn, becoming semi-conscious, restless. He tossed and turned in bed, occasionally lurching. Following the good doctor's suggestion, Paul slowly, peacefully died at home in his own bed wearing a morphine patch. It proved a comfort to me that I had known what was coming for almost a year.

Paul's old buddy, James Dickey, telephoned and wrote me a letter expressing his sorrow to not be able to attend Paul's memorial service on the farm. Paul and Jim went back to 1959, in New York, when they both read their poems at the 92nd Street Y. Dickey himself would die only a few months later, but his letter was urgent, telling me how time he had spent with Paul in his high-rise apartment was as close to heaven as anything he had experienced. He asked me "to stay in touch, so that we may be with Paul on both sides of the shadow-line. One can do such things, as you know."

Well, I didn't know, but I was soon to find out.

It happened on a fine February morning in the mountains, five months after Paul's death. Sunlight streamed through my yoga teacher, Joanne's window, a prism casting lively rainbows across the room as we side-stepped, loosened our bodies before yoga class. Despite consoling from hospice ladies, I had chosen yoga instead of the grieving class they offered. I decided my body rather than my mind was the path to peace. Suddenly, my teacher Joanne halted her stretching. She looked up at me and asked where was everyone? We were alone in the room where there should be seven other students.

Then she asked me if I had been dreaming of Paul. Tears suddenly welled up as I told her that yes, I had. I dreamt he asked me to move his ashes. Joanne silently left the room returning with a crystal from a collection in her bedroom, and slowly sat down while holding the crystal against her throat. Joanne was quite remarkable and well known in our mountain community for her psychic abilities. What she and I knew was that I also had my own psychic experiences starting when I was nineteen and feeling electricity coming up my legs while standing in a New England grave yard with headstones from the Revolutionary and Civil War veterans.

"No, I don't think that is his intention," she said slowly, eyes shut. Suddenly, she spoke as if she began to speak for Paul. "He has been with a group somewhere, and they are working together on their individual problems and to save the earth. He has chosen to leave them to come here, today, to see you."

During my lonely grieving, sitting in a large old farmhouse, I sometimes felt I could sense Paul's presence. Now hearing her words, I feel a twinge of fear. But who could have guessed or imagined what would now happen? In the next instant, I saw a sphere of light in the room, glowing white and fuchsia. Was this Paul's spirit? Was Paul now light energy? How was I supposed to understand what's happening? This brilliant image stayed briefly and then vanished. Although Joanne didn't see this light image, as I did, I noticed she was intent on something, her eyes closed as if she was carefully listening. Then she exclaimed:

"He wants to leave here with you, right now!"

She and I grabbed each other, crying. What was happened was beyond anything we had ever experienced or dreamt of. Then, acting on her words, I—or, Paul and myself, we both— left her house, when I remembered Paul had told me the meaning of a slang expression from his Navy days. When a sailor said "he had his ashes hauled," that meant having sex. How amazing, I thought, desire might exist even in the afterlife. It was marvelous but strange. Could Paul travel, filled with fuchsia-colored desire, from somewhere, back to see me? Once he'd written to me in a poem:

"You are where I belong!"

In the years since that incredible experience, I have shared it, cautiously, with a few people. Consequently, I've found others who had lived through, not the exact experience, but something similar. A documentary filmmaker wanted to use Paul's biography for his next project and told me he had always been an atheist. He never believed in the afterlife. When he read my account of my contact with Paul he found it matched what his wife's mother experienced after her husband had died.

Quantum physics currently tells of subatomic particles which when correlated communicate across the entire width of the universe. Are there some loves so intense they resonate after death?

Rose, ink, pastel drawing, 2015. Maryrose Carroll

Song for a Dead Lover, 1

And our world began with a big, big bang...

Cascading, tumbling our course to earth—not together
creations of merging ancestral genes
we floated through separate birth canals
seventeen years apart.

And the sun shines down on everyone...

We didn't know our wholeness surrendered to gravity's pull
peeling away connecting rites of power.
How could we know we had landed squarely on earth's surface
the way a voyager capsule returns from space.

And the sun recedes as stars began to shine...

Astounded eyes gaped at shapes and colors
just formed fingers grasped a breast.
fluid flowed through distinctly shaped bodies
pulled down by a gravity we couldn't see.

"For the rain it raineth every day..."

It was fifty years into your life, thirty-three mine
before we inevitably met. Memories
of another world now lost and forgotten
we moved to the beat of this planet.

And the wind blows through the city...

Ushered to our destinies by invisible African
Gods one fine May evening
we stepped into a gallery, halted by a crush of people.

And invisible birds trill their songs...

Side-stepping African art bound to be connoisseurs
of each other, our endless voyage
began with diner a movie and the blush-pink
and golden peaches waiting on my round table.

And trees in the park swayed...

As your gear moved permanently to my river loft
and stayed, while we honeymooned
through Rome, Paris, London, and Edinburgh
traveling by rail, plane, and van.

And the Romans shouted in train stations...

As we made our pilgrimage south to Ferlinghetti's
Big Sur where a clogged cabin chimney,
fire detritus left by Jack Kerouac forsake us
shivering while we tried to sleep.

And the ocean cracked and crashed against the shore...

Just as the sluice gates of joy opened in crept
terrors of childhood's fiercest
memories as you skidded to a slough of solitary sorrow
edging out love poetry existence.

"For the rain it raineth every day..."

Marrow deep, mother medusa memories
sent at fourteen, shriveling
in   a   sanatorium   with   old   coughing-bath-robed-men

spewing germs until sent home to a dying father.

And the leaves fall, pushed down by rain...

I bundled you down a spiral staircase thin
yet a heavy load.
Drove you to a doctor evading the edge of
doom—ordered into a hospital.

And the vain airedale chases the cat...

We who had loved at first sight now returned to our accord .
Home once more in our river loft no
discomfort cold, or toxic air, nor factory noise could distract
our scrutiny of the sweetest peaches.

The slick siamese turns, chases the squawking dog...

Then began our second honeymoon as you biked
to teach, to the park to pluck lines of poetry
out of the bushes, while I cut, ground, welded metal into
trees that won't grow leaves.

Just as the youngest cherries fall early from the tree...

Newly purged, the spark of fire rekindled in our eyes
fueled our progress, was our fiercest muse—
love, poetry and sculpture.

So, the fuller, rounder, ruby red cherries fall last.

Quotations

"For the rain it raineth every day..."
William Shakespeare, from *Twelfth Night*

Wedding Cake Dream
For Beth Sampson and Eric VanDemark

My eyes are birds darting into Treasure Island, past
a pink Charcuterie pig painting
Across the room I see diminutive, bald, Paul, hiding
behind mounds of red-blushed mangos.

Smelling excitement in the air—Carnival, the Fourth of July.
I try to reach, to catch him
bumbling past apricots, plums, pears stacked high
precise pyramids blocking my view.

Catching sight of him bounding up the stairway and
following soon seeing floor to ceiling
cereal boxes—terrific tony tigers in my way—cardboard
barricades, until jumping up seeing him.

Bald Paul is bounding up the next flight of stairs
to a floor filled with Warhol brillo boxes
laundry detergent promising fresher, whiter whites
arriving—he's not here.

I pass through the open door of a tiny top floor room
There lying in bed coyly he is
with the covers thrown back,
winking Me—I wake up

My bed is on fire!

Conversations with a Dead Lover, 2.

Twenty years since you walked with meat and marrow.
How can I ask you, my walking encyclopedia
about another sculptor, Socrates and his friend, Aspasia
Was she was his teacher?

   and Wiki's Socrates is a classical philosopher...

Love, not caught in the grasp of time and space, not earthy
speak of your interest in fiscal cycles.
Share your view broader than mine, of events that
lift lives up, pull them down.

   And the clock on the wall goes tick, tock, tock...

While a streamlet in Tbillis overruns its banks
floods a zoo releasing lions, and tigers and
bears to roam free, terrorizing Georgian citizens, even
a hippo tramps the highway.

   And "the rain it raineth everyday..."

These fringed-wing-butterflies, little commas fly north
to Edinburgh, pushed by weather
changes and their cousins, large blues are reintroduced
to Devonshire plain.

   And the butterflies flutter country to country...

"Joy delights in joy," as you soar among well-tuned spirits

While I lumber, bonking into Greece's crisis
sweating unseasonably here, in normally cool mountains
sun searing us relentlessly.

And sweat runs down the middle of my back...

I dream someone throwing a bucket of water on me—Ah,
how cool it would be dissolve
me down to curled toes—wicked witch of the east leaving
ruby red slippers.

And I would fly away, over the rainbow...

But magic water hasn't descended and I'm stuck sipping
my wine alone, watching my once
neat waist spreading like butter while trying to imagine
you—pure energy, memory, and mind.

And you fly somewhere...

While I muck out barns, repair the bridge,
voraciously cut weeds, again,
and again, and again their tenacious growth encouraged
by the rain.

I just think about my baby...

And wake each morning hugging the pillow
with-no-face,
sipping my coffee loving these green mountains
engulfing my senses.

And you tell me nothing of that other land...

Hollering noises assail my ears, the guy upstairs rants
that my dog is worthless
because an intruder entered, stole his shirts, forgetting

he left them in my washing machine.

And the money markets rise or fall...

Dumb-founded by his rage I imagine him a dark cloud swiftly drifting away while I
play the old pensioner's game, hobbling around
on stiff knees.

Pills plow through my shelves...

As the creek chirps, singing its Little Beaver Dam
song like Benny Goodman.
Can you hear it in worlds beyond? With the
music of the spheres?

Listen to the one who brings all this love...

The blue herons have withdrawn, occasionally
fishing below our bridge. then
flying silently filling the sky with their enormous
wings, kingfishers chattering loudly.

Who are you gathering with in that world beyond

Rumi, Shakespeare, Emily Dickson?
Surely present in the
Inn of the Poets in the Clouds joking, filling the air with their joy
joyfully in their company

And Will passes around the wine flagon...

Do all of you discuss, in iambic pentameter or in rhyme how to
help the distressed world
you left behind? Do you work, a Saul Bellow: with living beings,
those "grainfields" you visit?

Quotations:

and the rain it raineth every day... *Twevleth Night,* William Shakespeare
Joy delights in joy... *Sonnet Eight,* William Shakepeare
I just think about my baby... Andrew Hozier Byrne
Listen to the one who brings all this love... Elton John

Conversations with a Dead Lover, 3.

Buying breakfast from Miller's restaurant,

I move a mile to pick up feed
from Miller's feed supply—horses munch on baled hay
from grandma Miller's land.

And this country world winds intricately in circles...

From Dallas, a handsome eighty-nine, sends me the photo
of his majestic wife on arm
as they walk the march, his grandson's wedding
happy as any two might ever be

"Here comes the bride, here comes the bride"...

My sister in Phoenix goes out with her tennis player
ninety-three, in his new Cadillac
to find a movie theater with a parking deck where the
car won't be hellish-hot after the show

To Kill a Mockingbird is now Go Set a Watchman...

Here in the mountains we learn that the fossil fuel
industry received a trillion in
tax breaks, loans and subsidies from our government
war readiness in the Middle East.

Somewhere sustainable energy...

Beirut refuge women act in the play, Antigone, a
role they own in life
unable to find and bury their brothers
four million of them, forced to be actors in civil war.

"Why can't we be friends, why can't we be friends"...

I drive mountain roads in my forty-miles-a-gallon Fit
roads pristine from bombs, shelling
framed with forests, pastures,
drenched in mountain green laurel fueled by rain

And "the rain it raineth every day"...

Queen Anne's lace, white clusters, flowers with umbrellas
spines holding them in a hemisphere
freely spread themselves byzantine jewelry on leggy stalks around
the mid-summer green of our blessed land

"The best things in life are free"...

Tall wands of purple liatris blazing star attracting a
busy traffic of bees, butterflies
hummingbirds hovering about their gently waving stalks set
amid yellow-maroon, butterfly gladiolas.

The flowers in spring, the robins that sing...

The horses are heading back to the shade of the barn their
Black skins soaking up sun like sunflowers
my niece sitting in the shade of the chestnut tree asks
"Do bees sweat, Auntie?"

"Be My Little Baby Bumble Bee"...

We oscillate between thunderstorms pissing through the middle of
summer and sizzling-steamy weather

A perfect storm in western rivers is killing trout and salmon
low water levels and hotter summer heat.

"A voice cries out in the wilderness"...

Where are our heros. Can you spy a Washington or Jefferson in sight?
They were slave owners father of slaves
who nonetheless sent us in the right direction—equality.
Are we rolling down the hill, into muck?

Let the Goddess of Liberty return once more...

Every state has a story. A governor in jail blacks killed
by white police education bills
ignored forest fires dancing along freeways setting
cars and trucks on fire

And the leaders with vision?

My hospital friend whispers she thinks the fabric of society is
unraveling, after I give her communion
my insurance agent agrees worries about his grandchildren's lives.
What will they be like?

"Till the storm passes by"...

The new world fear is not vampires but migrants seeking a life risking
their lives to escape by any desperate
means from war, hostilities, crippling home circumstances threatening
homeland stability wherever they arrive.

"Whatever is said or done returns at last to me"...

Some call as weeds, stalks as lovey as Queen Anne's lace,.
welcome, I say, to my garden.
other plants, convovulvus, invade, take over, push out other flowers
all gardens must be weeded!

Make our garden grow...

Schools ended, a remote Volta River village in Ghana
the only white faced weed
I was humbled during their ceremony seated on the ground
we passed a bottle of schnapps.

When people lived in small villages and took care of each other...

each sipping passing pouring giving
a portion into the ground
back to what nurtures us our dusky
mother

"Still love...it's magnificent mountains"...

plants, watered, sending their roots deeper
crossing stabilizing the
ground reaching to the inner core beneath
where we stand

Quotations

Here comes the bride, here comes the bride... Richard Wagner—
   Bridal Chorus
Why can't we be friends, why can't we be friends... Charles Miller,
   Gerald Goldstein, Harold Brown, Howard Scott Lee Levitin,
   Lonnie Jordan, Morris Dickerson, Thomas Allen.
*The best things in life are free... The flowers in spring, the robins that
   sing...* Harris, james samuel lewis, terry/bivins, michael
Be My Little Baby Bumble Bee... Doris Day
till the storm passes... Mosie Lister
Whatever is said or done returns at... Walt Whitman
A voice cries out in the wilderness... Isiah

Earth Shivers

Stand Still! Feel the Earth
under your feet?

Electrified currents reaching up
your knees, groin, heart

Are you in a hallowed New England
cemetery with little flags

Revolutionary and Civil War dead
snuffed out in their time

Duress, pain, anxiety
energy that hasn't yet subsided

A slaving castle on Ghana's coast
with 200-year-old vibrations from

19,000 slaves stockpiled below my feet
for passage their new oppression,

something so horrific pushes the limit
every ounce of human energy

Song for our Earth

Praise to the Earth—"we ourselves are dust of the Earth"

Climbing a mountain road after morning rain
lightly lifted, last night's sweet scents
not yet washed away. seasonably late for honey locust
maybe a species yet unnamed?

"Our dead never forget this beautiful work that gave them being"...

Thinking we control by cataloging—from kingdom to subphylum
without Allen Ginsberg sacred communion
with brother and sister plants our family members creating these woods.

The dead "still love its verdant valleys, its murmuring rivers"...

This land was first 4 billion years before humans
Grenville mountain exposures flowing
like lava beneath the Appalachian mountains along this creek
my 70 years merely a flyspeck.

"Still love...its magnificent mountains, sequestered vales" ...

In a remote river area of Ghana humbly watching a ceremony
one white face present seated in a tribal circle
passing between us a bottle of schnapps, sipping each pouring
a portion into the ground.

Giving back to what nurtures us...

Muddy waters rising in Beaver Dam Creek rock-crushing
bluster around bound for New Orleans till
one day flowing back around to the Chicago River Lake Michigan and
eventually the Indian Ocean.

Praise be the fathomless universe...

Waters return as water circulating into the sky destined for
North Carolina, not California where
homes, cars, trucks, burst in flames for lack of water,
and too much heat.

Let it rain, let it rain...

Like an improbable bumble bee hanging like a mountain climber
upside down from a yellow touch-me-not
we cling to our paper rafts pretending they can float
on the rising oceans.

The world we have received also belongs to those who will follow us...

Reddish-brown stems nodding with blackberries, half red, half black
offer me breakfast while I walk up the mountain
with the dog following his pointer nose leaping through
bramble brush like brer rabbit.

Zip-a-dee-doo-dah, zip-a-dee-day...

Flowers prancing day and night furling and unfurling their petals
extending pollen laden stamens
for the delight of butterflies, hummingbirds, bees and myself
Please give them guardians to protect them!

This world needs bee guardians...

Willing slaves hives moved from pesticide filled field.
Millions hunting pollen, enabling our crops

returning disabled, vulnerable to varroa mites infesting their
commercially celled hives.

Unthinkable, a world without a sound of bees or birds...

Zipping down Bethel Road past fields tilted
walls of summer's green,
my car alone I slow for a logging truck stacked with
muscular trunks of poplar.

Drinking lots of soda pop, and that's not all...

Hemlock piled up thrice as high as orderly
rows of nearby corn
swinging, swaying on the curves
headed for saw mill

Amber fields of grain ...

It's a delicate balance—regular maintenance preventing weeds
grounding out strangling the charge
on wire strings keeping one thousand pound horses
in their pastures.

I'll bet my money on the bobtail nag...

Mare and filly range feeding and fertilizing
as they go black pasture ornaments
so beautiful to watch, while mowing grass these self-fueled
munching mowing hervibores.

Humans-animal bond beginning 50,000 years ago...

It's a still, silent war the planet our home is waging against us
at the very same time it feeds and sustains us.
No banners, flags waving, nor drumming, a marching band
just floods fires and drought.

Mother Nature is going to get you, if you don't watch out...

In Iran near the Persian Gulf it may no longer matter whether
you are Sunni, Shite or Israeli
when the temperature index rises to 163 more Syrians
drop of heat than civil war.

Stifling. This day is stifling...

Waking to steady pecking one two three of the woodpecker
gathering a feast for its brood.
Mason bee larva tucked inside the porch fascia trim If only
Mother Earth could peck out our dilemmas.

The young and swelling moon swimming in the west...

That the Earth is a living organism I have no doubt and being conscious
it has a memory I choose to live in land
with little bloodshed where the animals range freely grazing
while they wait for the farmer's offering of hay.

I believe a leaf of grass is no less than the journey work of the stars...

Treasure-traveling our mountain roads, I'm looking at cattle hugging the
ground before
the rain arrives. My car startles a young deer
white heart leaping up the bank, sheltered behind a tree it turns
to look at me, large, dark questioning eyes.

The poetry of earth is never dead...

Walking with my dog up the mountain road blazing color catches my eye
trailing white flowers a net of imperial red leaves
passed by thrill me with the sight. A woodsman tells me that these
are new sourwood trees their fragrance smelled weeks ago.

Fragrant lily-of-the-valley trees...

I've seen the alligator hide of mature sourwood trees up in the old forest
have these young ones walked
down the mountain starting a new prominent stand?
The bees will love them!

The Bees Trees sing together...

Perhaps the earth intuited how I love sourwood trees
arranged a present for me,
waving a hint with perfume wafted weeks
before I saw them.

There remains the song that names the earth...

Waving love air-borne sourwood sacraments, ritually combating
dumped trash and deafening sonar in the seas
I try to appease our sweetest earth swatting us with increasing
tornadoes hurricanes and heat.

Nobody knows the trouble I've seen....

While my hound dog walks me down the mountain my eyes
blistered by the view on the opposite ridge
ghost sentinels of hemlocks sucked of their green flying bits
of fluff wooly adelgid bugs.

all men and women of good will...

Vote heart hand and money not for limitless expansion of endless,
useless things the newest IPhone a bigger
car more meat to eat—edging out burning old growth more
plastic bottles bags to clog the guts of turtles.

Send a love letter to the earth...

Are we daughters and sons of the earth and sky? Do we think

we could live inside a laboratory bottle?
Lear-like have we given our power away lost our birthright
to know walk in salute and love the earth?

"We are already the past we become..."

Quotations

we ourselves are dust of the earth... Genesis, 2-7
The world we have received also belongs to those who will follow us...
    Chief Seattle
Still love...its magnificent mountains, sequestered vales... Chief Seattle
Our dead never forget this beautiful work that gave them being...
    Chief Seattle
Zip-a-dee-doo-dah, zip-a-dee-day... Ray Gilbert
Amber fields of grain... Katharine Lee Bates
I'll bet my money on the bobtail nag... Stephen C. Foster
The young and swelling moon swimming in the west... Walt Whitman
I believe a leaf of grass is no less than the journey work of the stars...
    Walt Whitman
The poetry of earth is never dead... John Keats
There remains the song that names the earth... Heidegger
Nobody knows the trouble I've seen... African-American Spiritual
We are already the past we become... Jorge Luis Borges

Dorothy Jane Finnegan. Edward Groth. 1927

To My Dear Unknown Ancestors

White dime-size dandruff
failing from cherry trees
ground carpeting by barn

Our task finished
so we drop into the earth
take our place

Ancestors
know I exist!

The mirror never lies
my mother's eyes
my father's mouth

Shadow figures behind
grandparents never met.

Violet. Maryrose Carrol, 2015

Slippery Path

Not dark yet a slippery path past early morning light
on powder blue snow
Listen—the steadying grain grinding
this black Tennessee Walker.
Subtract—150 years, spying through
barn board's gap
to shoot a bushwhacker
lusting for this mare.

My wooly path a thread dangling from
the click-clack of my mother needles
dropping into the basket by her feet Irish
sweater skills carried forth from Kerry.
Add—families braving the Atlantic
Those 19th century migrants.

A Song for Manufacturing

Endless cars counting voices reach ninety-nine as we wait for the train to pass. Clack-clack clacking of steel wheels, steel rails, red lights flashing, ding-ding-dinging bell.

SOS, Southern Pacific, Wabash Cannonball passing sleepy villages, hauling coal to feed the fires. At last, red caboose and guard arms rise to salute—Oh, mighty manufacturing power!

Where are the humming spinning furniture plants? On vacation— Mexico or China? In their luggage nuggets of strength, pride, wealth. Sad plants sadder villagers left behind.

Where is the steam calliope industry whistling pumping steam factory music white clouds steam rising into American's skies over Ford's River Rouge

Columbia Georgia's mills cotton white steam clouds. The American machine millions of hands, arms, legs

Wide-open pastel skies Goodyear turns cotton into tires. Steam clouds over Tacoma machinery for paper pulp production

White clouds grazed over rows—white refrigerators and first-time owners. An era remembered

Now calliope rusts plants shut. Workers try to move on or rust like their old tools.

Ode to All Workers

Here's a riddle—who caught on fire one night,
leaving 100,000 homeless, burning every   wooden building
to the ground?
St. Louis, New York,
and London sent help.

        "read the bones that dance after death…"

Who also rebuilt in stone and brick in three years,   employing masses
of masons architects,   setting the style
for new architecture?

        "very sweet, very nice on the empty box…"

Everything and everybody is moving in Chicago   this morning.
Planes buses trucks cabs.   Not to
mention the people moving   luggage food
passengers.

        "Its load of rocking dice…"

Writers writing editors editing Chicago
humming moving serving people crates of food,   spinning out
to airport.

        Wagon wheels wagon wheels keep on a turning…"

Nothing standing still except homeless camped on concrete
boulevards hugging cardboard belongings   44,000
                                                           in LA alone.

Quotations

Jacques Prévert, Sir. Herbert Read, Eddie Arnold

Is It Hate?

What freezes the heart   like eating polar ice cream?
Disconnects our wedding   with all living things
Leaves us stomping on   he ground below
forgetting it's not support   it's our prehistoric mother
As we Chew-Choo steam   through our smoke stacks
Or stage step, Punch and   Judy slugging all around

Does it start with a slap   or knife to the groin
Some say you have   to be taught to hate
But can it come in the   aggregate of daily shames
          "Don't speak your native tongue"
          "There is no work for you people"
Seeping through our memory   ancestors delegated to a heap bin
Shorn of hope dignity pride   outcasts even as they try to love
Circles kicked out of kilter   even before we are born Collide
with more of the same   below our feet
topsy earth cycles   recycle pain
          Whole countries locked into a dance of oblivion

Lily. Maryrose Carroll, 2001

Is It Love?

You would say Paul there doesn't have to be anything at all—
nothing.

> *"sans teeth, sans eyes, sans taste, sans everything..."*

No sky stars star consciousness no wind sun warmth or love.

> *"Seeing, hearing, feeling, are miracles, and each part and
> tag of me is a miracle..."*

No exotic evenings sharing wine food talk,
kissing exploring extending loving all night.

> *"fly me to the moon, let me play among the stars..."*

I can't imagine not existing my mind balks at any
understanding.

> *Is not existing better than living...*

Thinking we own this world as a birth rite   we have trouble
recognizing our place.

> *An instant survey—where do humans fit into the scheme of*
25

things...

We can't preserve the air or seas.
We help shove tons of plastic into turtles' guts We contaminate
water.

> *Such a sublime, scuzzy piece of work*

As Jacques Cousteau, observing ocean degradation predicted
decades ago,

> *the earth will do fine without us.*

Your ashes Paul confined to a metal box inside a wall cannot
contain your spirit as you tell me you are trying to help the earth.

> "*the love that moves the sun and the other stars...*"

Quotation

Paradiso, Dante Alleghieri
sans teeth, sans eyes, sans taste, sans everything... William
    Shakespeare
*Seeing, hearing, feeling, are miracles, and each part and tag of me is a
    miracle...* Walt Whitman
fly me to the moon, let me play among the stars... Bart Howard

Queen Anne's Lace. Maryrose Carroll, 2015

God Bless the Child

I bowed to her sitting
between my legs
fingers grazing her sunny hair

Saffron sun-drenched curls
grandpa's thick mop
her—not me—nor her sister

And what did we get from
grandpa's side
any better than life itself?

God bless the child who's got their own
that long thin line in red,
endless tribe hidden in our blood

A secret handshake
joining all my kin
whether dressed in silk or tatters

Be Lord High Mayor
haughty with
cascading chains and floppy hat

Or black draped widow-maker
with a singing sword
waiting to lop off heads

My lease to plant my feet
on the face of earth
was paid with their survival

Whatever their color, grace, or sins
each lived, passed on
those sacred genes

I bless each and every one.
I bless them all
for allowing me to be

Graced with an inexhaustible love for her legendary husband, poet Paul Carroll, **Maryrose Carroll** shares memories and her musical bonds about this love which continues beyond death. A love which James Dickey wrote her on Paul's death—allows us to "be with Paul on both sides of the shadow line."

The poems in this debut collection sprouted out, like water from a spring, after she finished her first book, *BEATS ME*, a telling of their life together and Paul's success in battling attempted censorship by the US Post Office when he published new writing by Jack Kerouac, Allen Ginsberg, and Wm. S. Burroughs in 1959. *BEATS ME* was selected as one of The Notable 100 Indie Books, 2015 by *Shelf Unlimited Magazine*.

Conversations with a Dead Lover fell immediately into a pattern, quatrains punctuated with a refrain, almost as lyrics. Her musical style preceded the Nobel Prize award to Bob Dylan, and indeed, Paul Carroll had attempted to recognize Dylan as a poet, in 1968, by inviting him to be part of the publication of *Young American Poets*.

Earl LeClaire has noted that in Maryrose Carroll's *Conversations of a Dead Lover,* "the poems are at once, a mystery, a love story and a blend of observations and explorations that pull us into uncharted waters." While a North Carolina Poet Laureate, Joseph Bathanti wrote "This is a book of breathtaking candor, the poet's seemingly limitless threshold for apprehending a love intensely physical, but also mystical, of another plane, of nuanced touch and texture, a love that accrues only by abiding the earth's lore and orbit, yet reckons that unseen world beyond our ken.

Maryrose has also been awarded as a "Runner-Up, 2016 Best Indie Book by *Shelf Unbound Magazine* for publishing *God & Other Poems, the Final Poems,* written by her husband, Paul Carroll, in the last ten weeks of his life.

A sculptor for four decades she has sculpted very large (up to 45 feet tall) public sculptures permanently sited in San Diego, River Grove, and Springfield, Illinois as well as Charlotte, Hickory, and Fayetteville, North Carolina.

She is currently writing a book of humorous vignettes: *Shall We Laugh? Wouldn't You Rather?* She moved, with Paul Carroll, from Chicago to a farm tucked in the Appalachian Mountains spitting distance from Tennessee and NC State Park, Grandfather Mountain, near Linville, North Carolina.

Her poetry reading tours have included The Poetry Center in Chicago, and libraries and coffee shops in North Carolina.

CPSIA information can be obtained
at www.ICGtesting.com
Printed in the USA
BVOW03s0256080717
488794BV00001B/3/P